WHY DID
THE RESURRECTION
HAPPEN?

DANIKA COOLEY

CF4KIDS

10 9 8 7 6 5 4 3 2 1
Copyright © Danika Cooley 2025
Paperback ISBN: 978-1-5271-1281-0
ebook ISBN: 978-1-5271-1338-1

Published by
Christian Focus Publications,
Geanies House, Fearn, Tain, Ross-shire,
IV20 1TW, Scotland, U.K.
www.christianfocus.com
email: info@christianfocus.com

Printed and bound by Bell and Bain, Glasgow

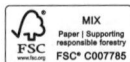

MIX
Paper | Supporting
responsible forestry
FSC® C007785

Cover design by Catriona Mackenzie
Illustrations by Martyn Smith

TABLE OF CONTENTS

Dedication

To the Reader (That's you!)
May you be a part of the great harvest of
Jesus' followers.

THE AUTHOR

Danika Cooley and her husband, Ed, are committed to leading their children to live for the glory of God. Danika has a passion for equipping parents to teach the Bible and Christian history to their kids. She is the author of *Help Your Kids Learn and Love the Bible*; *When Lightning Struck!: The Story of Martin Luther*; *Bible Investigators: Creation*; *Wonderfully Made: God's Story of Life from Conception to Birth*, and the *Who, What, Why?* series about the history of our faith. Danika's three year Bible survey curriculum, Bible Road Trip™, is used by families around the world. Weekly, she encourages tens of thousands of parents to intentionally raise biblically literate children. Danika is a homeschool mother of four with a Bachelor of Arts degree from the University of Washington. Find her at ThinkingKidsBlog.org.

THE FEAST
THAT POINTED TO THE RESURRECTION

Gardens are special places. God designed them to sleep every year while the weather is cold, and snow or morning frost covers the ground. Then when the weather warms, the snow melts, the morning frost turns to dew, and the trees begin to flower. Birds chirp, frogs sing, and plants burst out of the earth.

Today, most of us purchase our food from the grocery store. Even if it is frozen where you live, somewhere in the world apples and wheat are growing, ready to be shipped to hungry mouths around the globe. In the days of God's prophet Moses, that was not the case. The people of Israel were overjoyed when their gardens began to show signs of fruit and vegetables appearing.

During the Exodus, God instituted a number of feasts for his people to celebrate when they reached the Promised Land. The feasts helped the Israelites remember God's great blessings on them as he led them out of slavery in the land of Egypt. The feasts also pointed forward to the coming of Jesus, the Lamb of God, who would one day die on the Cross to take the punishment for the sins of all who believed in him.

The Feast of the Firstfruits took place at the beginning of the harvest. The people would bring the first sheaf of wheat to the priest at the tabernacle or, later, the temple. A sheaf is a bunch of wheat stalks tied together in a bundle. On the day after the Sabbath, our Sunday, the priest would wave the sheaf up and down to show that the person bringing the wheat was offering the very first part of their harvest that year to God.

The person bringing the offering would also give a gift of grain and wine, then sacrifice a perfect-year-old male lamb to show their gratitude to God. Until the Feast of the Firstfruits took place, the people of Israel did not eat anything from their harvest. So, they remembered that every good thing in their lives, including the harvest, came from God. By giving the first part of their harvest back to God, the Israelites glorified—honored and worshiped—him in their hearts.

Everything in the Bible is part of a grand story that God tells us about who he is, about who we are and why we need a Savior, about his plan for salvation, and about Jesus' commands to his followers. You see, God is good and holy and just. There is nothing sinful in God. But, Adam and Eve sinned in the Garden of Eden when they rebelled against God by disobeying him and eating the fruit of the tree of the knowledge of good and evil. That's when sin and death entered God's perfect world.

Humans have been sinning ever since. Romans 3:23 says, "for all have sinned and fall short of the glory of God." Our sin is a very sad thing. For, sin separates us from God and the punishment for sin is death. Yet, God had a plan for his people from the very beginning. He sent Jesus, who is the Son of God, to die on the Cross. That's where Jesus took the punishment for the sins of all who:

- Believe in him.

- Confess their belief with their mouths.

- Repent of—that means turn away from—their sin.

Now, the day Jesus died on the Cross was a sad day in history. Jesus, who is fully God and fully human, came to free us from sin. He did that by dying, which is terribly sad. Then, three days later, on Sunday morning, Jesus rose from the dead, which was exceedingly miraculous.

The Old Testament always points forward to God's great plan for our salvation through Jesus, God the Son. In 1 Corinthians 15:20-26, the apostle Paul showed how the Feast of the Firstfruits pointed to Jesus' resurrection. He wrote: "But in fact Christ has been raised from the dead, the firstfruits of those who have fallen asleep. For as by a man came death, by a man has come also the resurrection of the dead. For as in Adam all die, so also in Christ shall all be made alive. But each in his own order: Christ the firstfruits, then at his coming those who belong to Christ. Then comes the end, when he delivers the kingdom to God the Father after destroying every rule and every authority and power. For he must reign until he has put all his enemies under his feet. The last enemy to be destroyed is death."

You see, God gave his people the Feast of the Firstfruits to celebrate God's blessing of the harvest. Jesus is the beginning of the harvest for the kingdom of God. Though Adam brought death into the world, Jesus has made it possible for us to live eternally with him. When Jesus rose from the dead, he proved that he had conquered sin and death on the Cross. His resurrection showed that he paid the punishment for our sins.

There were many witnesses to the resurrection of Jesus. In fact, there were over five hundred witnesses. Everyone who believes in and follows Jesus will one day be resurrected just as Jesus was. Then, believers will live for all of eternity with Jesus. We will see and live with him, follow him in victory and live with him on the new earth where there will be no sin, no death, and no tears. Today, we are his witnesses as we share about his crucifixion and resurrection with our friends, family members, and the people we meet.

WHAT ARE FIRSTFRUITS?

The word firstfruits means the first of the fruits—or grain, or vegetables—from the harvest. Paul refers to Jesus as the firstfruits of those who have fallen asleep. "Those who have fallen asleep" means people who have died. One day, all who believe in Jesus will be raised from the dead, just as he was.

The Bible also tells us that Jesus is the beginning of the harvest. He is the firstfruits—the first of God's people to be raised and given a glorified spiritual body. Believers, too, will one day receive a perfect spiritual body—we are the harvest. At Easter—Resurrection Sunday, we celebrate God's good gift of the resurrection, the day when Jesus was the beginning of the harvest.

THE BEGINNING
OF THE HARVEST

To truly understand Jesus, you must know that there is only one God of the Universe. Also, our one God is God in three Persons. There is God the Father, God the Son—who is Jesus, and God the Holy Spirit. All three Persons of God are still just one God. We call this the Trinity. Now, Jesus—God the Son—was present at the creation of the earth. He was there when Adam sinned. Jesus was present when Moses spoke to the burning bush, too.

The apostle Paul wrote about Jesus in Colossians 1:15-18, "He is the image of the invisible God, the firstborn of all creation. For by him all things were created, in heaven and on earth, visible and invisible, whether thrones or dominions or rulers or authorities—all things were created through him and for him. And he is before all things, and in him all things hold together. And he is the head of the body, the church. He is the beginning, the firstborn from the dead, that in everything he might be preeminent."

To be preeminent means to be the most important—ahead of all others. That's what Jesus is. He is amazing. Jesus created all things, even angels, and he holds all things together. Jesus is also the head of the church—his people here on earth. Not only that, but Jesus is also the beginning of the harvest. He is the firstfruits, the firstborn of the dead—the first raised to eternal life with a forever body.

Jesus was born on earth, fully God and fully man, for a special mission only he could accomplish. You see, only a perfect, sinless man could take the punishment of our sins on himself. Not one of us is without sin, so we cannot save ourselves.

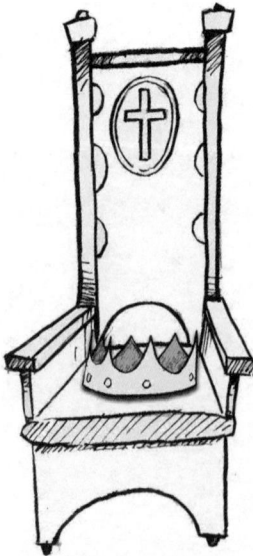

But, Jesus is God the Son, and he was born to live a perfect, sinless life so that he could take the punishment for our sin. Jesus was innocent of any charge against him. Yet, the Jewish religious leaders and the Roman officials had him killed. Roman soldiers beat, whipped, and spit on Jesus, then mocked him. They even made a crown out of thorns and pushed it onto his head. Then, they crucified him.

During the crucifixion, God showed his power through several amazing acts. First, the entire earth turned pitch black as if the sun had died for three hours, beginning at noon when the sun was at its brightest. Jesus died, proclaiming, "It is finished." His mission to free us from our sins was accomplished. Then, the curtain into the temple's Most High Place was torn in two, and a massive earthquake split rocks in half.

Last, to show God's power over death, many tombs were opened, and those who had believed in God's promise of Jesus' coming were raised to life. They walked out of their tombs, entered Jerusalem, and were with people in town for the Passover feast. Can you imagine denying that Jesus is the Son of God after witnessing all that? Still, there were people with hard hearts who refused to believe.

After Jesus' death, two believers named Joseph of Arimathea and Nicodemus wrapped his body in linen cloths covered in aloe oils and myrrh. They laid Jesus' tightly-wrapped body in a new tomb that had been created for Joseph. We know from archaeology that the tomb would have been cut into the side of a stone wall, with a pit in the center of the small cave. Stone benches would have been carved on each side of the

pit, and they would have placed Jesus' body on one of these benches. Most tombs from that time had square stones that were shoved into the opening, but Joseph was very rich, so he had a special rolling stone that covered the entrance to the tomb.

Because Jesus had been telling people that he would be killed then raised three days later, the Jewish religious leaders placed Roman soldiers to guard the grave and sealed the stone so that no one could slip into or out of the tomb. Jesus didn't need to sneak out of the tomb. His disciples didn't need to steal his body to make it seem like Jesus had been telling the truth about his resurrection, either. You see, on Sunday morning the seal was broken, and the stone was rolled away. The guards were absolutely terrified.

When Jesus rose from the dead, he proved beyond any shadow of a doubt that he had conquered sin and death on the Cross. Three days after Jesus died to pay for our sins, a spectacular miracle happened when Jesus was raised from the dead. If we follow Jesus, we can trust that our sins are paid for. His resurrection is the proof.

Now you know that Jesus is the firstfruits, the first of a great harvest for the kingdom of God. When Jesus rose from the dead, he received a new, incorruptible, forever body. Incorruptible means that his eternal body will never get sick, or old, or die. Our bodies now are fragile, like jars of clay. In eternity, we will have bodies that will never break or get hurt—they will be made to last for all eternity.

One day, Jesus will return for his people, and everyone who believes in him will receive a new incorruptible body, too. Jesus' resurrection guarantees that, just like Jesus, in eternity we will never get sick, or old, or die. In fact, we will live forever with Jesus on the new earth, where there will be no sin and no death.

PEOPLE RAISED FROM THE DEAD IN SCRIPTURE

Scripture tells true stories of people raised from the dead to show God's power. Once, the prophet Elijah asked God to raise a widow's son, so the boy came to life. Later, the prophet Elisha prayed over the body of a boy who sneezed seven times then opened his eyes. God brought a dead man to his feet after his body was thrown into Elisha's grave, touching his bones.

Jesus woke a dead man in front of his mother. To Jairus' dead daughter, Jesus said, "Child, arise," and she did. Lazarus was dead for three days when Jesus called him out of the grave. These people later died, but when Jesus returns in victory, they will be raised into their new bodies.

WITNESSES
AT THE TOMB

In a court of law, a witness is someone who gives testimony to an event they saw happen, or to what happened afterward. Testimony is a written or spoken statement that gives all the facts so that others will know what happened, too. That way, the people in the courtroom hearing the testimony of the witness can understand what has occurred. In the Jewish courts, God required that there be at least two or three witnesses to an event in order for their testimonies to be considered valid and true.

When Jesus died on the Cross, real people in history witnessed it. There were also many witnesses to his resurrection. In fact, over five hundred people saw Jesus risen, and alive, at one time. Sometimes Jesus even spoke and ate with people after his resurrection.

Naturally, people in Jerusalem hearing that Jesus was alive may have questioned the resurrection. After all, they didn't see the risen Jesus themselves. But anyone who heard the stories of Jesus' resurrection also knew exactly where Jesus' tomb was. Skeptics could easily walk out to the gravesite and verify that Jesus' tomb was, indeed, empty. Even better, they could question the witnesses and hear their stories for themselves.

Immediately after Jesus rose from the dead, the empty tomb was witnessed by Roman guards, by a group of women, and by Peter and John. Even the Jewish religious leaders knew the tomb was empty.

The Guards and the Chief Priests

Do you remember that the Jewish religious leaders set guards at the tomb and sealed the stone? Well, these precautions did not stop Jesus from rising from the dead—not at all. A tremendous earthquake shook the ground at dawn on Sunday morning. Then, an angel of the Lord, who looked like lightning with snow-white clothing, rolled the stone back and sat on it. That is exactly what the big, tough guards saw

occur. Naturally, they were terrified. They shook so hard that they appeared to be like dead men. When some of the women who traveled with Jesus showed up with spices for his body, they found him gone. The women spoke to the angel before running off, and the guards watched it all happen.

Being a guard was an important job. Knowing they could be sentenced to death for losing the body of Jesus—who was now very much alive, some of the guards ran to tell the chief priests the whole story. Now, the priests could have cried out to God and grieved, repenting for killing the Son of God. Instead, they gathered the elders together and decided to

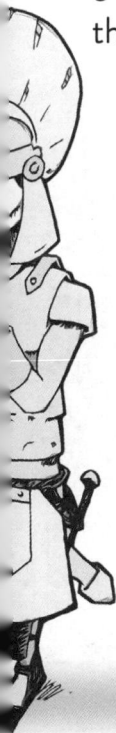

lie. So, the Jewish religious leaders bribed the guards with money and told them to tell people that Jesus' disciples stole his body while they were sleeping. That is just what the guards did—they lied.

The Women

When you think about Jesus' ministry, do you envision him traveling with just his twelve disciples? Jesus often went to private places so he could teach just the Twelve, but there were actually many people who followed him. In fact, there were a number of women who traveled with Jesus and his followers. These believing women funded his ministry and cared for the needs of Jesus and the twelve disciples. Did

you know that at least two of the disciples' mothers traveled with Jesus?

At the Cross, John and his mother, Salome, witnessed Jesus' death. Jesus looked down and asked John to care for his mother, Mary, who was also present. There were more women at the Cross, too. Mary Magdalene, the sister of Martha and of Lazarus whom Jesus raised from the dead, stood by watching. Yet another Mary, the mother of Joses and of Jesus' disciple James the Younger, was a witness to the crucifixion. Joanna, the wife of Chuza, the manager of Herod of Galilee's household, also came to be with Jesus that day.

At dawn on Sunday morning, Mary Magdalene, Mary the mother of James, Salome, Joanna, and the other women took spices and went to the tomb. Like the guards, they, too, witnessed the angel who looked like lightning. "Don't be afraid," said the angel, for that is what angels who look like lightning say to terrified humans in the stories throughout Scripture. "You are looking for Jesus. He isn't here. He has risen, just as he said he would. Go tell the disciples."

Of course, the women ran from the tomb. They accidentally raced straight into Jesus, who was very much alive. The women fell to the ground and

worshiped Jesus, which is the right thing to do when you meet God the Son on the road. Jesus told them to go tell his brothers—the disciples—to go to Galilee, for he would meet them there (Matthew 28:9-10).

Peter and John

Mary Magdalene ran to tell Peter and John that Jesus was not in the tomb. Of course, Jesus' friends wanted to see this for themselves, so they ran to the gravesite. Along the way, they started to race. John made sure that he wrote in his eyewitness testimony of Jesus' life, death, and resurrection that he won the race. At the grave, John stooped down to look inside

the tomb entrance. The linen cloths Jesus had been wrapped in were there, lying on the bench.

Catching up, Peter barged right past John into the empty tomb. The cloth that had been over Jesus' face was neatly folded on the bench next to his abandoned linens. John followed Peter into the tomb to look around. There was no body at all. Because of all that he had seen, John believed that Jesus was risen from the dead. So, Peter and John left.

THE CREED OF THE WITNESSES

A creed is a statement of beliefs. Christians memorized and passed around a creed of the early church, which Paul wrote down in 1 Corinthians 15:3-8. The first two verses say: "For I delivered to you as of first importance what I also received: that Christ died for our sins in accordance with the Scriptures, that he was buried, that he was raised on the third day in accordance with the Scriptures..."

Paul passed on the creed without changing it, including the fact that the Bible points to Jesus' resurrection. The creed also lists people who witnessed the risen Jesus, whom Paul described by writing, "most of whom are still alive" (v. 6). The witnesses were alive—available to give testimony.

JESUS WENT
BEFORE US

Just as witnesses in a court of law testify about what they have seen, witnesses to the risen Jesus testified about seeing Jesus alive. Jesus remained on earth for forty days, appearing to witnesses and preparing his disciples for ministry. You see, the eleven remaining disciples became Jesus' apostles. He sent them out to

tell others the good news of the gospel so they, too, could be saved from their sins.

Luke, a doctor friend of the apostle Paul's, wrote the book called "The Acts of the Apostles," a history of the early church. In Acts we learn that Paul was not among the original twelve disciples. Instead, Jesus chose Paul to be an apostle later. In fact, Paul had been a Pharisee—one of the elite Jewish religious leaders. Before Jesus appeared to Paul and called him to be an apostle, Paul persecuted Christians.

Luke wrote in Acts that as Jesus appeared to the disciples over a period of forty days, he gave commands to the eleven apostles and taught them more about the kingdom of God. Jesus also told his friends to remain in Jerusalem, waiting for the baptism of the Holy Spirit. After Jesus rose to heaven, God the Holy Spirit did come to the early church at the Feast of Pentecost in Jerusalem during an exciting event you can read about in Acts chapter two.

So, forty days after Jesus rose from the dead, he met with his disciples on the Mount of Olives above

the village of Bethany, where Mary Magdalene, Martha, and Lazarus lived. On the mountain with Jesus, the disciples asked him about this kingdom he had been teaching them about. Specifically, they wanted to know when the kingdom would be restored to Israel. You see, the disciples seemed to believe that Jesus would make everything here on earth as it was when King David ruled Israel. Maybe they hoped God would send a great army to overthrow Rome so that Israel's leaders could finally, once again, rule over their own people.

So, what is God's kingdom? The kingdom of God, which the Bible also calls the kingdom of heaven, is the splendid kingdom God rules over. One day, all of God's people from every nation and every time throughout history will gather together for all of eternity. If you are a Christian, you are already a part of the kingdom of God and you will live forever with Jesus on the new earth.

Instead of answering the disciples' question about when Jesus would restore Israel to glory, Jesus changed the subject. He said, "It is not for you to know times or seasons that the Father has fixed by his own authority. But you will receive power when the Holy Spirit has come upon you, and you will be my witnesses in Jerusalem and in all Judea and Samaria, and to the end of the earth" (Acts 1:7-8).

Jesus instructed the disciples to tell others about the miraculous things Jesus did. They would explain that every one of us has sinned and that our rebellion has offended our holy God. Then, they would tell people that Jesus died on the Cross to take the place of everyone who believes in him and repents. You see, Jesus died as a substitute for each believer, taking the punishment for their sin. Next, the disciples would tell people that Jesus rose from the dead, which proves that his work on the Cross truly did free sinners from their sin.

So that is exactly what the disciples did. They were witnesses to Jesus, and because of their testimony many people were saved. Those new believers became a part of the kingdom of God for all eternity. One day, you and I will meet them. Until then, it is our job to tell others about Jesus, too.

After Jesus told the disciples to be his witnesses to people in Jerusalem, Judea, Samaria, and the ends of the earth, he ascended to heaven. The word ascend isn't one we use very often, but it means to rise up. That is exactly what Jesus did. He lifted his hands and blessed his beloved friends. Then, he was lifted up into heaven. Naturally, the disciples had never seen anything like this happen before! They stood like statues, watching their Savior rise into God's throne room until he was covered by a cloud.

Suddenly, two men dressed in white were speaking to them. "Men of Galilee," the angels said, "why do you stand looking into heaven? This Jesus, who was taken up from you into heaven, will come in the same way as you saw him go into heaven" (Acts 1:11). So, the disciples worshiped Jesus, God the Son, and returned to Jerusalem. While waiting for Jesus to send the Holy Spirit to them, they stayed in the temple, praising God.

It is important to know that Jesus rose from the dead in a glorified spiritual body, so he will always be fully

God and fully man. When Jesus rose into heaven— the place God created as his throne room—Jesus was seated at the right hand of the Father. In fact, he still is. Because he loves us, Jesus is constantly asking God the Father to give us everything we need while we are here on earth.

Jesus went before us into eternity with the Father. He is the firstfruits of those who have risen from the dead. The spirits of those who die before Jesus returns will wait in heaven with him. You'll read all about that in the chapter "Jesus is Returning". Then one day, Jesus will return and everyone who belongs to Christ, from throughout history, will live forever, just like Jesus. Those who have already died will be resurrected.

MARCHING ORDERS FROM JESUS

Have you heard about the Great Commission? A commission is a command someone in charge gives to his people. After the resurrection, the eleven disciples met Jesus on the mountain and worshiped him.

Then, Jesus gave them this commission: "All authority in heaven and on Earth has been given to me. Go therefore and make disciples of all nations, baptizing them in the name of the Father and of the Son and of the Holy Spirit, teaching them to observe all that I have commanded you. And behold, I am with you always, to the end of the age" (Matthew 28:18-20).

Christians are to make disciples of all people, to baptize them in the name of our Triune God, and to teach them Jesus' commands.

JESUS APPEARS
TO THE DISCIPLES

Seeing the risen Jesus changed everything for the disciples. Rather than hiding from their enemies in the upper room, they went out and shared the good news of the gospel of Jesus with them. The disciples-turned-apostles founded churches and taught others to be disciples of Jesus. The disciples actually were in danger, but they only cared about inviting new people to join the kingdom of God. They were so certain Jesus is the Son of God that every disciple, except John who was exiled, willingly died for the sake of the gospel.

The Road to Emmaus

After the crucifixion, Jesus' eleven disciples remained in Jerusalem. Other followers of Jesus returned to their homes in other villages. As Cleopas trudged the dusty walk home from Jerusalem to the village of Emmaus with his friend, their hearts were heavy.

Along the way, a stranger approached them on the road and asked what they were talking about. Cleopas said, "You were in Jerusalem—and you don't know what happened there?" The man asked the two friends what had occurred.

They replied, "Jesus of Nazareth was a mighty prophet of God. Our chief priests and religious leaders turned him over to the Romans to be sentenced to death and then they crucified him." Now the men took a breath and betrayed their doubt. "We hoped Jesus was the one to save Israel. Today is the third day—some of the women who have traveled with us went to the tomb. They said they saw angels and that

the tomb was empty. The women said Jesus is alive."

Now, the stranger said, "O foolish ones, and slow of heart to believe all that the prophets have spoken! Was it not necessary that the Christ should suffer these things and enter into his glory?" (Luke 24:25-26). Then, the man explained all the things in Scripture that pointed to Jesus.

There were no restaurants in those days, so Cleopas and his friend invited their fellow traveler to dinner. The man thanked God for the bread and broke it. As he handed it to them, God opened their eyes and they realized this wasn't a stranger at all. They'd been talking

to Jesus all along. Then, Jesus vanished. So the men ran all the way back to Jerusalem, found the disciples and their friends and told them, "The Lord has risen indeed!"

The Twelve-Now-Eleven

Cleopas and his friends were telling the disciples, who met behind locked doors, what happened. Suddenly, Jesus himself stood in the middle of their gathering. Of course, the disciples and all their friends were terrified. They thought maybe they were seeing a spirit.

Jesus asked his friends why they were afraid and doubtful. "See my hands and my feet, that it is I myself. Touch me, and see," he said. "For a spirit does not have flesh and bones as you see that I have" (Luke 42:39). Jesus wanted the disciples to know he was not a spirit, so after he showed them his hands and feet, he asked them for food and ate a piece of broiled fish in front of them.

Then, Jesus explained to his closest followers all the ways that the writings of Moses, God's prophets,

and the poetry of the Psalms pointed to his death and resurrection. He told them they were witnesses to all these things and instructed them to stay in Jerusalem. For, Jesus was going to send the Holy Spirit to his people.

Jesus' disciple Thomas wasn't in the locked room when Jesus came, so he declared he would not believe Jesus was alive unless he put his fingers into the scars created by the nails in Jesus' wrists, which the ancient Jews referred to as a part of the hand, or into Jesus' side where the guard had pierced him with a sword.

Eight days later, Thomas and the rest of the disciples were behind a locked door when Jesus suddenly stood with them. Jesus told Thomas to put his finger in his hands, and his hand in his side. "Believe," he said. Thomas cried out, "My Lord and my God!"

That is exactly right—Jesus is our Lord and our God. Then, Jesus said that those who have not yet seen him risen from the dead with their eyes, but believe in him anyway are blessed. Do you believe in Jesus Christ as your Lord and Savior? If so, this blessing is for you!

The Five Hundred

In 1 Corinthians 15:3-8—the creed of the witnesses—verses 5 and 6 say: "...and that he appeared to Cephas, then to the twelve. Then he appeared to more than five hundred brothers at one time, most of whom are still alive, though some have fallen asleep." Who was Cephas? Well, Jesus renamed Simon, his disciple, Peter. The word Peter in Greek means *rock*. In Aramaic the word rock is *cephas*. So, Cephas is the Aramaic way to refer to Simon Peter.

Paul also tells us that Jesus appeared to over five hundred brothers in Christ at one time. Some people think this happened on the mountain in Galilee while Jesus gave the Great Commission. Really, we don't know when or where it happened. We just know it occurred because the Bible tells us it did. Sometimes God doesn't supply a lot of details about an event.

Now, five hundred men are a lot of witnesses. When Paul wrote his witness creed, he told the church at Corinth that most of the witnesses were still alive. People could easily go talk to the people who had seen Jesus raised from the dead, just like they could go and see his empty tomb. Everyone knew the resurrection really, truly happened. In fact, people they knew had witnessed Jesus alive.

WHAT HAPPENS WHEN WE FALL ASLEEP?

In 1 Corinthians 15:20, Paul wrote, "But in fact Christ has been raised from the dead, the firstfruits of those who have fallen asleep." Those who have "fallen asleep" means people who have died. For Christians, death is temporary because all Christians will be raised when Jesus returns. So, for believers, death is like sleeping.

So, what happens when someone dies? Their body sleeps in the grave while their spirit is in heaven. While we are in our body on earth now, we can pray and talk to Jesus and hear from him as we read his Word, but we do not see him physically. In the final resurrection, Jesus will return from heaven. In 2 Corinthians 5:8b, Paul wrote, "we would rather be away from the body and at home with the Lord."

JESUS IS
RETURNING

After Jesus ascended to heaven, do you remember what the angels said to the disciples? Jesus' followers were staring at the clouds when the angels said, "This Jesus, who was taken up from you into heaven, will come in the same way as you saw him go into heaven" (Acts 1:11b). It is wonderful news that Jesus is returning for his people.

In 1 Corinthians 15:20, Paul wrote, "But in fact Christ has been raised from the dead, the firstfruits of those who have fallen asleep." Do you remember that Old Testament believers celebrated each new harvest by giving God the firstfruits—the first of their harvest? The feast pointed forward to the resurrection of Jesus, who was the first to be raised to eternal life. You see, Jesus is the first of a mighty harvest for the kingdom of God. In 1 Corinthians 15:21-23, Paul told us, "For as by a man came death, by a man has come also the resurrection of the dead. For as in Adam all die, so also in Christ shall all be made alive. But each in his own order: Christ the firstfruits, then at his coming those who belong to Christ."

You remember that Adam brought sin and death into the world through his rebellion against God. Because of Adam's sin, everyone dies—or falls asleep —for a time. You remember, too, that Jesus was raised from the dead, which means that every person who believes in Jesus, confesses that belief with their mouth, and turns from sin to follow Jesus, will also be resurrected. You also know that until Jesus returns, the spirits of those who have died will be with Jesus in heaven while their bodies rest—or sleep—in the grave.

Then, when Jesus returns, all believers get brand new eternal bodies—that will be the harvest that follows Jesus' resurrection.

Do you ever wonder what happens to people whose bodies can't sleep in the grave because they die at sea, or in a fire, or are ill, or are somehow harmed? There is no need for concern, because God doesn't need our old bodies to be intact in order to give us new forever bodies. God will create just the right body—a new body—for each one of us to live in forever. Although Christians have burials to show our respect for the

bodies God gave us and to bear witness to our faith that one day we will receive a new forever body, our burials are just a symbol of our faith.

Have you ever been to a funeral or memorial service? Maybe you saw people cry. Perhaps you cried yourself. When people we love are asleep in Christ, we miss seeing them. It hurts knowing we will not visit with our loved ones until Jesus returns. We can take great comfort in God's promises, however. We don't need to be afraid of our own death, either. After all, for a Christian death is only temporary.

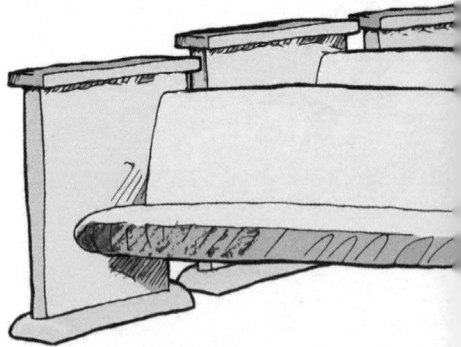

When Paul wrote his first letter to the believers at Thessalonica in Macedonia, he said, "But we do not want you to be uninformed, brothers, about those who are asleep, that you may not grieve as others do who have no hope" (1 Thessalonians 4:13). We don't grieve without hope because we know that Jesus died and rose again. Paul also wrote, "We would rather be away from the body and at home with the Lord" (2 Corinthians 5:8b). Won't it be exciting to see Jesus face to face?

Since God will also raise all believers from the dead when Jesus returns, if someone you know has fallen

asleep in Jesus, you can pray. Tell Jesus when you feel sad. Then, thank him that one day you will spend all of eternity with your Christian loved one.

In 1 Corinthians 15:24-26, Paul wrote about Jesus, "Then comes the end, when he delivers the kingdom to God the Father after destroying every rule and every authority and power. For he must reign until he has put all his enemies under his feet. The last enemy to be destroyed is death." One day, Jesus will return and make all things right.

Until Jesus comes back, we live in the already-and-not-yet kingdom of God. What does that mean? That's a really good question.

The kingdom of God is already here. If we follow Jesus, we are already a part of God's family of believers. God is with us now, too. After Jesus ascended to heaven, he sent the Holy Spirit to dwell in the hearts of all who believe in him and repent. Jesus did not leave us alone on this earth—he is always with us.

So, we are already a part of God's kingdom, and Jesus Christ lives with us through the Holy Spirit. But, we are not yet in the complete, perfect kingdom of God. Jesus conquered sin and death on the Cross, but we still see people die here on earth. We still struggle with sin. One day, though, Jesus will return and he will

put all of his enemies under his feet. Jesus will crush death—no one will die ever again. That's really good news.

Until Jesus returns, we live in the already-and-not-yet kingdom. One day, we will have forever bodies, but not yet. We will never sin on the new earth, but we are not there yet. We will live with Jesus, but we don't see him with our eyes yet. One day, all things will be made right, but it hasn't happened yet.

Until Jesus returns, we live for Jesus here in the already-and-not-yet kingdom of God. You see, Jesus is already on his throne. He is already the King of the Universe, and he is in control of all things. We can trust Jesus because he is always good, always faithful, and he never changes. We don't need to be afraid because Jesus is always in control.

WHEN IS JESUS RETURNING?

Everyone wants to know when Jesus will return for his people. It's a good question, isn't it? Jesus' disciples thought so, and they asked him how they would know that he is returning.

Jesus told his disciples, "But concerning that day or that hour, no one knows, not even the angels in heaven, nor the Son, but only the Father. Be on guard, keep awake. For you do not know when the time will come" (Mark 13:32-33).

We don't know the day Jesus will return, but we know for certain that he will. So, we should live every day like it's the day Jesus may return. That means living according to Jesus' commands, avoiding temptation, serving God, and loving our neighbors.

MORE ELDERS
MEET THE RISEN JESUS

The creed of the witnesses ends in 1 Corinthians 15:7-8: "Then he appeared to James, then to all the apostles. Last of all, as to one untimely born, he appeared also to me." The apostle Paul is speaking of himself when he says "me." The amazing thing about Jesus' appearance to Paul is that it happened after Jesus ascended to heaven.

The early church was led by apostles, elders, and deacons. These men of God shared the gospel with unbelievers, preached God's Word, cared for widows and orphans, and discipled believers to follow Jesus as the church grew. They did other important things, too, like pointing out false teachers and prophets, who claimed to be speaking for Jesus, but who were really just teaching lies.

Matthias

After Jesus rose to heaven, his disciples and followers descended from the Mount of Olives and traveled through the village of Bethany to the upper room in

Jerusalem. The eleven remaining disciples-turned-apostles were Simon Peter and his brother Andrew, James and his brother John, Andrew, Philip, Nathanael, Thomas, Matthew, James the Younger, Simon the Zealot, and Judas (not Iscariot). Just twelve of Jesus' many followers had been chosen to be in his special inner circle.

Mary the mother of Jesus and Jesus' brothers were in the upper room, along with the women who traveled with Jesus during his ministry. Many of Jesus' other followers were there, too. Altogether, there were about 120 people gathered.

Jesus' twelfth disciple, Judas Iscariot, had betrayed Jesus as the Psalms prophesied he would. When Judas the Betrayer died, the disciples knew they needed to replace him. That was also a prophecy. Peter said the new apostle must be chosen from among the disciples who had followed Jesus from the time that John the Baptist baptized him until the ascension. The new apostle also must have witnessed the resurrected Jesus.

So, the church elders—leaders—decided between two men named Joseph and Matthias. The apostles wanted Jesus to choose the new apostle from his

throne in heaven, so they prayed and asked Jesus to show them who to choose. Then they cast lots, which were probably marked stones priests used to ask God for help making decisions. The lots pointed to Matthias, so he was made an apostle of Jesus.

Jesus' Brothers

After Jesus was born to Mary—a virgin—through the Holy Spirit, she married Joseph who became Jesus' adoptive earthly father, raising and caring for Jesus as a child. Then, Mary and Joseph had other children. Scripture tells us that Jesus had sisters along with four brothers named James, Joseph, Judas—or Jude, and Simon. At first, his brothers didn't think the boy they grew up with was the Messiah—the Christ, the Son of God. John wrote, "For not even his brothers believed in him" (John 7:5).

Jesus' brothers were in the upper room with the apostles after Jesus' ascension. They were a part of the 120 believers that gathered together. How did Jesus' brothers go from mocking him to believing he is the Christ?

In the creed, Paul wrote that Jesus' brother James witnessed Jesus alive and risen from the grave. Since the brothers of Jesus were all gathered together with the apostles, women, and many disciples of Jesus after his ascension, it makes sense to conclude that Joseph, Jude, and Simon also witnessed their brother rise into heaven. It changed their lives—and the church—forever.

James went on to write a book of the Bible. Jude, too, wrote a very short book of the Bible. In 1 Corinthians 9:5, Paul writes about apostles having the "right to take along a believing wife, as do the other apostles and the brothers of the Lord and Cephas." So, we know Jesus' brothers all had wives who traveled with them, sharing the gospel so that new people could be saved. Jesus' brothers became preachers after seeing him alive.

Paul

The early church was greatly persecuted by those who hated Jesus. At one point, the deacon Stephen was preaching when he was brought to stand trial before the Jewish religious leaders. They did not want to hear the truth about Jesus, so they killed Stephen. Yet, when Stephen was stoned to death for preaching the gospel, he was not afraid. You see, in Stephen's suffering, the Holy Spirit allowed Stephen to see into heaven. He saw the glory of God the Father, and Jesus standing at the Father's right hand.

Before stoning Stephen, the Pharisees threw their valuable cloaks at the feet of a young Pharisee. Paul, whose Jewish name was Saul, approved of Stephen's stoning. In fact, Saul became a terrible and vicious persecutor of the church. He would go house-to-house with his murderous thoughts, dragging Christian men and women from their homes and throwing them into prison.

On the way to Damascus to imprison more Christians, Saul was surrounded by a bright light from heaven. As he fell to the ground, he heard a voice say, "Saul, Saul, why are you persecuting me?" (Acts 9:4). Saul, who after this went by his Roman name Paul,

wrote that he had seen the risen Jesus. Paul asked, "Who are you, Lord?" Jesus replied, "I am Jesus, whom you are persecuting" (Acts 9:5). Jesus told Paul to rise and go into Damascus.

Paul spent three days blinded, and then Jesus sent him to see a Christian man, called Ananias, who healed Paul's eyes. Then, Jesus called Paul to be his apostle to the Gentiles, to kings, and to Israelites. That's how Paul, a persecutor of Christians, became a follower of the risen Jesus. He wrote thirteen books of the New Testament. In the end, he was executed for preaching the gospel.

WHAT IS AN APOSTLE?

The word apostle means one who is sent out. In the three years that Jesus traveled throughout Israel and the surrounding areas, many disciples followed him. Early in his ministry, Jesus handpicked twelve special disciples to become the foundation of the church.

When Jesus died and was resurrected, the eleven remaining disciples became apostles. Matthias replaced Judas Iscariot as one of the Twelve. Later, Jesus chose Paul to preach the good news of Jesus to the Gentiles and to the Jews. The Bible tells us that the apostles witnessed the risen Christ and were chosen by the Holy Spirit. Jesus' apostles were sent out by Jesus to build his church and performed signs and wonders in Jesus' name, for his glory.

THE NEW EARTH
AND THE FINAL
WITNESSES

In the beginning, there was no sin in God's perfect, very good world. It was a sad, sad day when sin and death entered the world after the first man and woman sinned. But God had a marvelous plan for our salvation. He was not at all surprised by our rebellion against him. In fact, he planned for it and made a way for us to be forgiven.

Do you remember what Paul wrote in 1 Corinthians 15:20-26? "But in fact Christ has been raised from the dead, the firstfruits of those who have fallen asleep. For as by a man came death, by a man has come also the resurrection of the dead. For as in Adam all die, so also in Christ shall all be made alive. But each in his own order: Christ the firstfruits, then at his coming those who belong to Christ. Then comes the end, when he delivers the kingdom to God the Father after destroying every rule and every authority and power. For he must reign until he has put all his enemies under his feet. The last enemy to be destroyed is death."

Jesus conquered sin and death on the Cross, but there is still sin in this world. We still see people die. We are living in the already-and-not-yet kingdom. One day, though, "not yet" will become "now."

On that day, Jesus will return and there will be a great war. "For they are demonic spirits, performing signs, who go abroad to the kings of the whole world, to assemble them for battle on the great day of God the Almighty" (Revelation 16:14). Jesus will win the final battle, then sin and death will be banished forever.

Jesus will bring all his people, in glorified bodies, to his Father. Finally, the kingdom of God will be gathered from people of every nation throughout all of history.

Then, God will give us an entirely new heaven and new earth, with a new Jerusalem, where no one has ever sinned. In a vision from God, the apostle John saw the new Jerusalem. He described it in Revelation chapters 21 and 22. Now, some Bible detectives—called theologians—think some of John's description is symbolism, while others believe that everything will be exactly as described. We probably can't begin to understand how marvelous our forever home will be.

You may notice some descriptions of the new Jerusalem sound like things that were described in the Garden of Eden, or in the tabernacle. That's because throughout the Old Testament God gave us shadows— representations of the true, eventual reality—to help us understand who he is and his great plan for salvation. Not one thing in the Bible is a mistake.

John describes the new Jerusalem, God's holy city, coming down from heaven. God announces, "Behold, the dwelling place of God is with man. He will dwell with them, and they will be his people, and God himself will be with them as their God. He will wipe away every tear from their eyes, and death shall be no more, neither shall there be mourning, nor crying, nor pain anymore, for the former things have passed away" (Revelation 21:3-4). What a wonderful place our new home will be.

The new Jerusalem, where God will dwell with us, will have a high wall made of jasper with an angel at each one of twelve pearl gates, and the names of the tribes of Israel will be written on each gate. There will be

twelve foundations for the twelve walls, and the twelve apostles' names will be inscribed on the foundations. The foundations will be decorated with beautiful jewels, like the high priest of Israel's breastplate once was. There will be jasper, sapphire, agate, emerald, onyx, carnelian, chrysolite, beryl, topaz, chrysoprase, jacinth, and amethyst.

The city itself will be made of sparkling gold with a gold street. The river of the water of life will flow from

the throne of God and the throne of the Lamb, Jesus. Growing along each side of the crystal clear river, the tree of life will offer twelve types of fruit—one for each month, with leaves that heal the nations.

In the new Jerusalem, there won't be a sun or moon. Rather, God himself will be our light and Jesus will be our lamp. There also won't be any night and the gates will never shut because there will be no need to protect us from evil. You see, the new Jerusalem will be a place without sin or danger. Because God will dwell with us, there will be no need for a temple.

Just as the followers of Jesus witnessed our risen King after the resurrection, we too will be eyewitnesses to our risen Lord. Christians have faith that, one day, we will follow Jesus in the harvest. We will have eternal, glorified bodies, and we will live forever with Jesus in the new Jerusalem, worshiping God forever and ever. Even though we do not see Jesus now, we have his Word—the Bible, and we can trust that everything he tells us is true.

Believers bear witness to Jesus during our lives now, telling friends, family members, and even strangers about the good news of Jesus Christ. We teach others about the disease of sin, about God's great plan for salvation, and that Jesus will return for his people. Finally, we share the gospel with our listeners, telling them that to be forgiven our sin for all eternity, we simply must believe in Jesus, confess our belief with our mouth, and repent of our sin. Then we, too, will be a part of God's kingdom. Have you put your trust in Jesus as your risen Savior? Now is a good time to talk to a parent or pastor about this.

HOW WILL WE KNOW IT IS TIME?

In ancient days, a king's people ran out of the walls of the city to meet him as he arrived home. Then, they ushered him into the city. When King Jesus returns, everyone will know.

Paul wrote, "For the Lord himself will descend from heaven with a cry of command, with the voice of an archangel, and with the sound of the trumpet of God. And the dead in Christ will rise first. Then we who are alive, who are left, will be caught up together with them in the clouds to meet the Lord in the air, and so we will always be with the Lord" (1 Thessalonians 4:16-17)." What a joyous day that will be!

TIMELINE

Before 4000 BC

- God creates the heavens and the earth.
- Satan tempts Eve and Adam. The Fall happens and sin enters the world.

1446 BC

The Israelites celebrate the first Passover and leave captivity in Egypt. *This is the early date for the Exodus.*

- God gives Moses instructions for the Feast of the Firstfruits.
- Note: The dating for the rule of Pharaohs in Ancient Egypt varies, as calendars varied. Also, there are two widely accepted dates for the Exodus. This timeline is based on the early date. The early date of the Exodus works backward from dates in Scripture, and is supported by many conservative scholars.

c. 6/4 BC

Jesus is born in Bethlehem.

AD 6

- The Roman Empire makes Judea a Roman province.
- Judas the Galilean leads the Zealots in an uprising against Roman taxes on Jewish citizens.

c. 28-29

John the Baptist ministers near the Jordan River. Several of the disciples, looking for the Messiah, spend time following John.

c. 28-30

- Jesus begins and works his public ministry, sharing the gospel, teaching disciples, and healing the sick.

- Jesus calls the Twelve Disciples to follow him.

c. 30

- Jesus is crucified. He is raised from the dead and forty days later, he ascends to heaven.

- Jesus' half brother James witnesses the risen Jesus and becomes a Christian.

- Jesus sends the Holy Spirit to the believers gathered at Jerusalem and Pentecost occurs. The apostles become witnesses to proclaim the gospel.

33/34

Jesus reveals himself to Paul on the way to Damascus and calls him to be an apostle to the nations.

36

Pilate is removed as governor due to incompetence.

40-45

James, the half brother of Jesus, writes a letter to Jewish believers scattered outside of Israel.

41-44

- Herod Agrippa, the grandson of Herod the Great, kills James the brother of John.

- Peter is imprisoned by Herod Agrippa.
- Herod Agrippa is killed by an angel of the Lord.

46-47

Paul goes on his first missionary journey.

48/49-51

Paul goes on his second missionary journey.

49-51

Paul writes 1 and 2 Thessalonians.

50-54

Peter comes to Rome.

51

Paul visits the church at Corinth.

52-57

Paul goes on his third missionary journey.

52-55

Paul ministers in Ephesus.

53-55

- Mark writes his Gospel, based on Peter's testimony.

- Matthew writes his Gospel.

- Paul writes 1 Corinthians while he is in Ephesus.

54-68

The reign of Roman Emperor Nero, who persecuted the church.

55-56

Paul writes 2 Corinthians while in Macedonia.

c. 55-57

Paul writes 1 Corinthians to the church at Corinth. At the time that he writes his letter, many of the 500 brothers Jesus appeared to are still alive.

57

Paul writes Romans from Corinth.

60-70

Hebrews is written by an unknown author.

62

- James, Jesus' half brother, is martyred by the Sadducee high priest, Ananas.

- Peter writes 1 Peter while in Rome.

- Paul writes Ephesians, Philippians, Colossians, Philemon, and Philemon while under arrest in Rome.

- Luke, Paul's doctor and traveling companion, writes the Gospel of Luke and Acts.

62-64

- Paul writes 1 Timothy from Macedonia.
- Paul writes Titus from Nicopolis.

64

The Roman Emperor Nero blames Christians for a massive fire in Rome and kills many believers.

64-67

- Peter writes 2 Peter.
- Jude, the half brother of Jesus, writes his letter.
- Paul writes 2 Timothy.
- Paul and Peter die for sake of the gospel in Rome.

70

The Roman army, under Emperor Titus, lays siege to Jerusalem for five months, murders the high priest Ananias, and destroys the temple.

79

Mount Vesuvius erupts and destroys Pompeii and Herculaneum.

81-95

The reign of Roman Emperor Domitian, who persecutes Christians.

9-95

John, the only apostle who is not martyred, writes 1-3 John and the Gospel of John, probably while in Ephesus.

95-96

John writes Revelation while exiled to the island of Patmos by Roman Emperor Domitian.

c. 100

John dies of old age on Patmos.

WORKS CONSULTED

Currid, John D. and David P. Barrett. *Crossway ESV Bible Atlas*. Crossway, 2010.

Dodson, Rhett P. *With a Mighty Triumph!: Christ's Resurrection and Ours*. The Banner of Truth Trust, 2021.

Elwell, Walter A. and Robert W. Yarbrough. "The Middle East in the Days of Jesus." *Encountering the New Testament: A Historical and Theological Survey, Fourth Edition*. Baker Academic, 2022.

Gribetz, Judah, Edward L. Greenstein, and Regina Stein. *The Timetables of Jewish History: A Chronology of the Most Important People and Events in Jewish History*. Simon & Schuster, 1993.

Grun, Bernard. *The Timetables of History, New 3rd. Rev. ed.* Simon & Schuster, 1991.

Haynes, Clarence L. Jr. "Who Were Mary and Joseph's Other Children?." *Bible Study Tools*, https://www.biblestudytools.com/bible-study/topical-studies/who-were-mary-and-josephs-other-children.html, March 5, 2024. Accessed May 6, 2024.

Packer, J.I. *What Did the Cross Achieve?* 1974. Crossway, 2023.

Piper, John. *Fifty Reasons Why Jesus Came to Die*. Crossway, 2006.

Rhodes, Jonty. *Man of Sorrows, King of Glory: What the Humiliation and Exaltation of Jesus Mean for Us*. Crossway, 2021.

Rose Book of Bible Charts, Maps & Time Lines. Rose Publishing, 2010.

Ryle, J.C. *The Cross: Crucified with Christ, and Christ Alive in Me.* 1852. Rev. ed., Aneko Press, 2019.

Sproul, R.C. *The Truth of the Cross.* Reformation Trust Publishing, 2007.

Stott, John. *The Cross of Christ.* 1986. Centennial ed., InterVarsity Press, 2021.

The ESV Study Bible™, ESV® Bible. Crossway, 2008.

"Was Matthias or Paul God's choice to replace Judas as the 12th apostle?." *Got Questions,* https://www.gotquestions.org/ Matthias-Judas-Paul.html. Accessed May 1, 2024.

"What is an Apostle?." *Got Questions,* https://www. gotquestions.org/what-is-an-apostle.html. Accessed May 1, 2024.

Other books in the Series

Why Did the Exodus Happen?
978-1-5271-1176-9

What was the Tabernacle?
978-1-5271-1175-2

Who was Moses?
978-1-5271-1174-5

Why Did Slavery End?
978-1-5271-1011-3

What was the Underground Railroad?
978-1-5271-1010-6

Who were the Abolitionists?
978-1-5271-1009-0

Why did the Reformation Happen?
978-1-5271-0652-9

What was the Gutenberg Bible?
978-1-5271-0651-2

Who was Martin Luther?
978-1-5271-0650-5

Who were the Disciples?
978-1-5271-1279-7

What was the Cross?
978-1-5271-1280-3

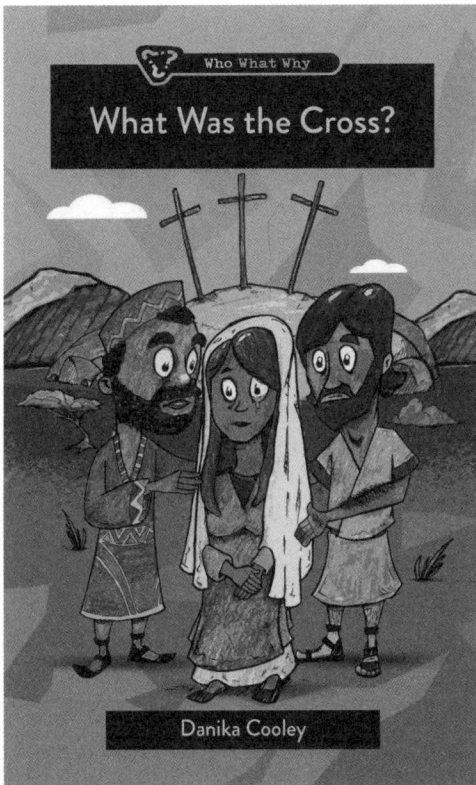

What Was the Cross?
Danika Cooley

Discover the amazing story of the Cross in this engaging book from the Who, What, Why? series! With fun black–and–white illustrations and easy–to–understand explanations, young readers journey from the Garden of Eden through God's incredible rescue plan to Jesus. Author Danika Cooley helps kids understand why the Cross is more than just a symbol as they meet fascinating Bible characters and watch God's plan unfold through history. Perfect for home, Sunday school, or family devotions!

ISBN: 978-1-5271-1280-3

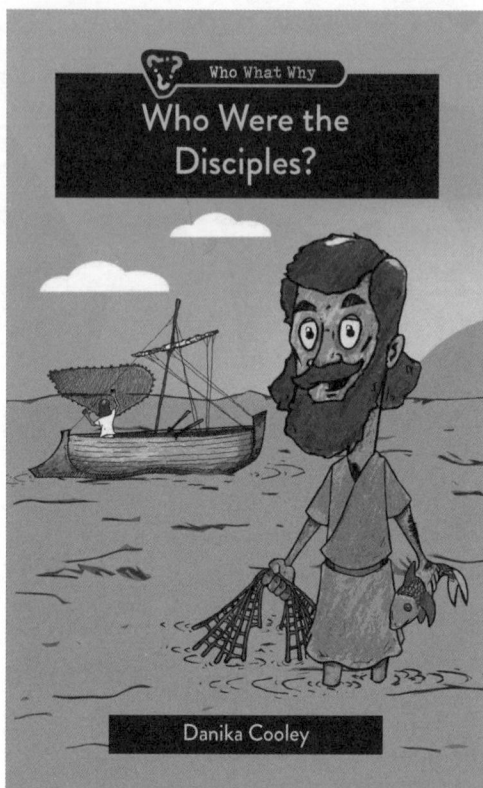

Who Were the Disciples?
Danika Cooley

Dive into the incredible true story of Jesus' twelve disciples – regular guys who became part of history's greatest adventure! From fishermen to tax collectors, these ordinary men were transformed into extraordinary followers who changed the world forever. With engaging black–and–white illustrations throughout, discover how Jesus' closest friends faced challenges, performed miracles, and spread the good news across the globe. Perfect for young readers who love history and adventure!

ISBN: 978-1-5271-1279-9

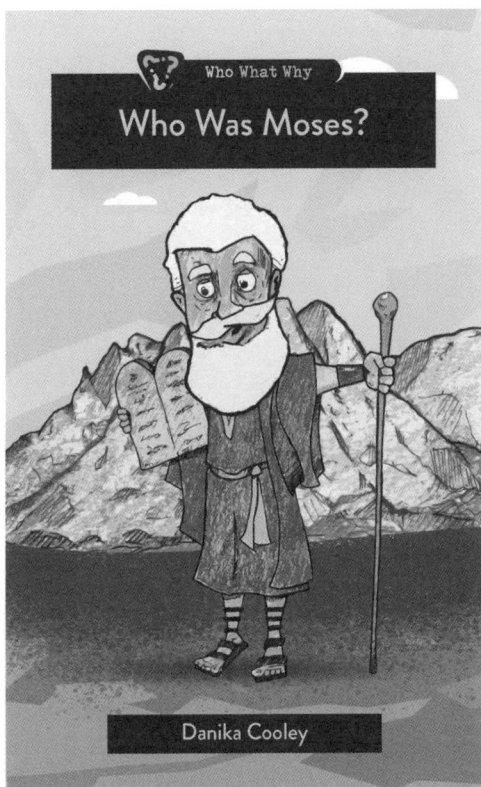

Who Was Moses?
Danika Cooley

From a baby born in slavery to a prince to an outlaw to the leader of God's people, Moses's story is an amazing one. Award–winning author and Bible curriculum developer Danika Cooley draws you into the twists and turns of Moses's life, and shows you how this flawed man was able to know God face–to–face. There are plenty of pictures and maps included, as well as a timeline to show how Moses's life fitted in with other events in history. The Who, What, Why series explores the lives, concepts, and movements that have shaped the lives of God's people throughout history.

ISBN: 978-1-5271-1174-5

Christian Focus Publications

Our mission statement
Staying Faithful

In dependence upon God we seek to impact the world through literature faithful to His infallible Word, the Bible. Our aim is to ensure that the Lord Jesus Christ is presented as the only hope to obtain forgiveness of sin, live a useful life and look forward to heaven with Him.

Our Books are published in four imprints:

⟨◯⟩ CHRISTIAN FOCUS

Popular works including biographies, commentaries, basic doctrine and Christian living.

⟨◯⟩ MENTOR

Books written at a level suitable for Bible College and seminary students, pastors, and other serious readers. The imprint includes commentaries, doctrinal studies, examination of current issues and church history.

⟨◯⟩ CHRISTIAN HERITAGE

Books representing some of the best material from the rich heritage of the church.

⟨◯⟩ CF4KIDS

Children's books for quality Bible teaching and for all age groups: Sunday school curriculum, puzzle and activity books; personal and family devotional titles, biographies and inspirational stories – because you are never too young to know Jesus!

Christian Focus Publications Ltd,
Geanies House, Fearn, Ross-shire,
IV20 1TW, Scotland, United Kingdom.
www.christianfocus.com